LEONARD RICHMOND

Landscape Painting
in Oils

Pitman Publishing Corporation • New York • London • Toronto

Introduction

The following are three basic guides for the student of landscape painting: 1) To understand the function of pictorial composition, it is necessary to study the pictures of established artists. 2) If a picture is to convey any sort of message, clearly it must have a definite groundwork on which the artist's feelings can be displayed. 3) The beginning landscape painter should paint only those subjects that can be approached directly as regards his own emotional reaction.

Pictures may be arranged in many ways. I strongly recommend the simplest basic design, so that when the painting is seen by others its pictorial intentions will be clearly understood. I have seen thousands of landscape pictures by inexperienced painters which would have benefited greatly from a coherent and understandable compositional basis to pull the subjects together.

I advise those who wish to become distinctive landscape painters to make as many outdoor studies as possible. The more information one absorbs about natural phenomena the better qualified he is to paint—either outdoors or in the studio. Ultimately, an original creation, your own conception, may be evolved. In the meantime painting should be enjoyed, and skill—or the lack of it—should not worry you. Paint boldly and freely. If you love color, show the world that you do love color. If you are after sensitive and subtle tones, develop the ability to express just that. And most important, never set about landscape painting unless there is a real urge to do so.

Cornfields

First Printing
Printed in The United States of America

Library of Congress Catalog Card Number 62-9137
Copyright © 1962 by Pitman Publishing Corporation

Planning the Picture

In arranging the composition of a picture one must very carefully observe the shapes of objects and study them in relation to other surrounding objects. Composition is a matter of organizing various shapes into a picture so that they form a harmonious whole. In order to see shapes in broad outline without being distracted by details, one should close his eyes half way.

The success of a picture lies in the clarity of its message to the beholder, and this can be achieved only by eliminating unnecessary material. To have two messages in one subject is confusing and often contradictory. While it is important that shapes be balanced, they do not at all need to be symmetrical; a large dark mass can be balanced against a small light one, and vice versa. As there are no fixed rules, composition is a matter of constant practice, and it is only through trial and error that beginners in outdoor sketching learn the correct placement of various items in the landscape.

The student should choose a subject that makes a good composition. An old cottage or a pretty stream, by itself, will not do unless it is organized with its surroundings to make a satisfactory whole. In other words, the scene may need rearranging —perhaps the addition of a tree or the relocation of a cottage— to improve the composition of the picture. It is advisable to try several ways of composing the subject and then to select the most suitable one.

Figure 1 shows the basic pattern of the colored reproduction (Plate I). The arrangement of contrasting light and shadow are clearly indicated. Notice how the surrounding dark foliage gives prominence to the centrally placed red building.

An important point to remember in composing a landscape is that the position of natural light and shadow changes rapidly. Even within an hour shadows are altered in shape. When beginning a sketch, therefore, place the shadows accurately and speedily and adhere to their original position throughout the painting.

Figure 1. (above). Basic Pattern of **Richmond Creek**
Figure 2. (below). First Stage of **Richmond Creek**

The tone values used in Figure 2 are mostly self-explanatory. The area space of the sky is small and of relative unimportance. It is therefore subordinated in tone value to the general surroundings so that the building, dark trees, and water reflections can convey their message with clarity.

Speaking generally, the landscape painting should be built up on four basic planes that clearly define, first, the foreground; second, the middle distance; third, the distance; and fourth, the sky. All colors used in the landscape must be arranged carefully with due regard to their correct tone values in relation to the picture as a whole.

Foreground objects assist in presenting the distance in its correct relative position. However, objects added pointlessly to the foreground will detract from the main statement of the picture.

In most landscapes the middle distance provides the principal interest, and the composition should be arranged so as to give it due prominence. The foreground lines should tend to lead the eye to the center of the design.

Depth may be achieved when middle distance and foreground are in contrasting tones. Where the foreground is in shadow and the middle distance brightly lit, the eye passes readily to the brighter parts of the composition.

Plate I.
Richmond Creek

Plate II.
The White Cottage

Intense colors should be used in the foreground of any picture —usually the actual colors of the objects; this is known as *local color*. The colors in the middle distance are not so strong and usually are mixed with gray, while those in the background, if distance is the desired effect, will be bluish in tone. An example of this use of color to indicate distance is seen in Plate X, "Landscape, Elizabethtown, N. Y.," shown on the last page of the book.

As in all outdoor scenes, the artist must assess the number of planes and tone values before he paints. The warm-colored cornfield in the foreground occupies about one fourth of the space area; its receding lines lead the eye to the farm buildings in the middle distance, which are dramatically emphasized by the dark trees behind them. The trees in turn lend the correct tone values to the blue mountains in the background; thus an effect of distance and depth is achieved.

In the colored reproduction entitled "The White Cottage" (Plate II), a dark shadow was placed behind the cottage. This enhanced the value of the sunlit foreground on the right. Little detail was used in the distant moors. When I was quite sure what the subject would be, the white cottage being the predominant theme, I made the background tonally quiet. In order to take its place in the general scene, the white cottage had to be treated so that the nearer foreground should echo the sunny effect of the cottage, thus isolating it from its surroundings.

Figure 3. First Stage of **The White Cottage**

Figure 4. A Surrey Farm

Figure 3 demonstrates that point. Notice that the light on the landscape behind the cottage on the right-hand side is too light in tone. Actually, this gave a keynote to the distribution of light spreading to the middle distance. By exaggerating the essentials of a scene of this type, one can paint the final stages with confidence.

Observe in Figure 4. "A Surrey Farm," how the direction of light spreads downward on the sloping farmhouse roof. The trees behind the building emphasize its structural formation and lend a framework to the farmhouse and its outbuildings. Notice how the darker trees, silhouetted against the sky, contrast in tone with the lighter-tinted trees or bushes. In the actual scene there were no light trees or shrubs in front of the dark group, but for the sake of composition they were put in to afford an agreeable contrast to the darker background.

"Surrey Farm" is a formalized pattern painted out of doors. The danger of studio composition is that one's ideas are prone to become stereotyped, so that one soon becomes afraid to take risks. Direct contact with nature stimulates the imagination to undertake original and fresh themes. It is always advisable, however, once you have made the plan of your picture, to stick to it. If you find as you develop the painting that you do not like it, it is better to start again than to alter the original plan; the latter would probably result in a loss of balance in your composition.

Tone Values

Perhaps the most important compositional aspect of landscape painting is tone value. Tone is the 'weight' of a color, the degree of darkness and lightness that it registers; it is divided into light, middle, and dark. In order to judge tone out of doors, close your eyes half way; you will then be able to get an over-all impression of the depth of the colors before you. When you are about half way through the painting, it is well to check its tone values using this method.

A failing of many amateur paintings is too much tonal attention to the sky, at the expense of the landscape below. The usual mistake in a sunny subject is to render the sky too light. Assuming that the artist succeeds in copying from nature a brilliant natural sunlight, it does not follow—for artistic reasons—that he should retain it in the final painting, since unity of tone of the whole picture must be the first consideration. If, in a landscape, the sky occupies a small area, it should be painted in a low key, as it is obviously of minor importance.

If the eye is attracted solely to the sky, the picture is bound to be a failure. Let us imagine that the subject is a sunlit bridge, occupying a prominent position in the general composition. It is important to bring the bridge vividly to the mind of the viewer. A sky painted light in tone would prove to be an opposing force to the sunlit bridge. The answer in such an instance is to subdue the tone of the sky, leave out clouds, paint simply, with little variation, and paint in gradated tones.

After completing an outdoor sketch I would suggest, as an exercise, painting the same scene again in a series of four gradated grays spreading from the darker foreground to the lighter distance and through to the sky. This would indicate the four basic planes, viz., foreground, middle distance, distance, and sky. Any detail added to the four gray planes automatically takes its place in the general setting of the picture. It also helps to assess the correct tone value of each item in the landscape. This sort of study gives the student a greater insight into the potentialities of the subject and also more confidence during the final painting.

The colored reproduction, "Landscape, New Mexico" (Plate III), shows a subject that suggests many possibilities in color and decoration. In the first stage, Figure 5, notice how the group of dark trees on the right helps to create a striking composition. The whole design was kept low in tone, so as to have the benefit, when working in the final stage, of painting a lighter tint over the dark ground with some certainty of success. To leave out the dark patch of trees on the left would have been fatal to the composition. Notice how the deep shadow of the trees on the right sweeps across the picture, leading the eye to the dark trees on the left.

Figure 5. First Stage of **Landscape, New Mexico**

Plate III.   Landscape, New Mexico

All of the first stage was painted very simply so that the design could speak for itself. The student should realize that he' must paint quickly in the first half hour, making a clear statement of the subject's fundamental pattern. In the finished picture, Plate III, the problem was to paint the green-tinted material on the hill without disturbing the general serenity of the picture in terms of tone value. The true artist is one who masters the tonal value of the whole picture, allowing no single element to disturb its balance. The two figures in the foreground on the left-hand side are valuable, since they add human interest to the general effect and also lend a sense of proportion to the over-all composition. The rock formation arising from the soil in the foreground adds to the brilliant effect of sparkling sunlight.

Figure 6, "Old Buildings, Elizabethtown, New York, "is a typical American rustic scene. This subject, also, was painted under bright sunny conditions. The composition is bold and entertaining. For the sake of design, the trees behind the building needed reorganizing. The dark fir tree behind the sunlit building was invaluable as a device for contrast.

A simple—and probably the best—method of painting trees is to render them at first in mass formation and flat in tone. Confusion often arises from too much detail in trees, destroying the essence of the subject. After completing the first stage, add interstices of light to the foliage on the wet surface. This will suggest naturalistic growth. Later the main trunk and branches can be added; those who enjoy depicting detail will find they have an excellent foundation on which to lay their final touches. It should be borne in mind, however, that whatever the result, it is essential to retain a pervading sense of tone.

In Figure 6 the sky, being lower in tone, prevented the trees from being too prominent and also helped to give brilliancy to the sunlit buildings and the road in the foreground. There are several ways of commencing an outdoor subject. In this instance the canvas was left untouched where the light caught various items—thus helping to suggest the brilliancy of sunlight. To enhance the value of the bright effect of light on the building and road, it was necessary to deepen the tone of the sky. This created a contrast that tends to lead the eye to the foreground. It was an all-important build-up toward a sound composition. As mentioned before, students are prone to painting skies too light in tone, thus losing the main feature of the landscape below. An awareness of this factor will be an invaluable aid to the beginning landscape artist.

Figure 6.   Old Buildings, Elizabethtown, New York

Color Composition

Just as tones may be classified as pale, middle, and dark, so colors may be classified as warm, cold, and neutral. Warm colors are yellow and red, and those near them; cold colors are blue, blue-green, and violet; neutral colors are black, white, and gray. Green is warm if yellow predominates, cool if blue predominates. When colors are diluted with a neutral color, they become less brilliant. So, if orange is diluted with white, it becomes a sort of salmon or flesh-pink; if it is mixed with black, it becomes a burnt sienna; if mixed with gray (i.e., both black and white) it becomes anything from brown to a warmish gray. In this way all the colors in a natural scene are brought into one frame of reference. The painter sees certain relationships between them.

Colors may be *complementary* to each other. That is, they are made up of opposite primary colors. Red is the complement of green (blue and yellow), and blue of orange (red and yellow). Complementary colors set each other off, and if placed side by side look more intense than when seen alone. Neutral colors provide contrast and set off brilliant colors effectively.

Plate IV.
Pescadero, California

In observing the natural color of objects the artist will find that the play of light causes different parts of their surface to vary as much in color as in depth of tone. Some of the variations are of the "local" or intrinsic color of the object, but these will not appear equally intense all over the object, since different parts of the surface catch different amounts of light. Other variations are owing to reflection. In this connection think of a lake reflecting blue sky or cloudy gray sky or brightly colored boats.

Once the painter becomes aware of the way his eyes react to the color of light, he will cease to look on the natural scene as being composed of separate objects in space, each one having its own isolated color; he will see it instead as a network of shimmering gradations. One color will have a little of every other color reflected in it.

When he tries to express his vision of radiant color, the artist meets certain difficulties. The first is with form: to interpret the brilliance of light, boundaries of form must be broken down to suggest the halo effect of objects in very bright light. Then there is the problem of adjusting the rival claims of color and tone: tone is a quantity of light, color a quality of light.

Accuracy of tone may to some extent have to be sacrificed when the painter is primarily concerned with interpreting natural color. He will not want to reduce the brilliance of his colors by mixing too much of the black element with them. When the expression of radiant color is desired, the artist is limited by the range of physically obtainable colors on his palette. He must therefore *suggest* brilliance rather than actually present it. The palette range is by no means as brilliant as the colors of the spectrum. Delacroix once defined a colorist as a man who could make brown paint look red by the colors he put next to it.

The colored reproduction entitled "Pescadero, California" (Plate IV) demonstrates a method of expressing radiant color. It is an outdoor study painted under ideal weather conditions. Although the area space of the blue sky is small compared to the landscape below, it affords a pleasant contrast to the warm-tinted hills and middle distance.

The oil painting entitled "The River Bouquet, Elizabethtown, New York" (Figure 7) is an interesting subject for two reasons. First, the massive boulders and rocks lend dignity and

Figure 7. The River Bouquet, Elizabethtown, New York

power to the composition; second, the deep-colored water—mostly amber in tint—is much darker in tone value than the adjoining rocks. In drawing and painting large rocks it is necessary to handle them decisively, so that they appear structurally solid. Occasional sharp edges or contours help to give solidity; strongly defined shadow, painted in deep-toned color, lends added substance to the weight and shape of a rock.

The first coat of color for the amber-tinted water was painted with burnt sienna, well diluted with turpentine. Before this was dry, veridian mixed with cadmium yellow (middle) was painted over most of the burnt sienna. The blend gave a sumptuous appearance. The color used for the bright sunlit foam—spreading horizontally across the picture—was made with a generous quantity of white mixed with a little yellow ochre. The less obvious touches of light on the water are mostly blue in tint. The secret for painting small elements like those in this picture is to use large brushes. Dark tones sometimes require two coats of paint, but students should try to paint color effects with one coat only.

Technique—Mountain Scenery

After selecting a suitable subject, students should make at least three small color studies out of doors—in addition to some pencil notes—for direct information. Later in the studio, using a large canvas, the student can devote himself freely to the actual painting with the help of these previous studies.

Each day, owing to the temperamental moods of nature, mountain scenes change in color and tone, though the basic structure of mountains is actually divorced from climatic conditions. In pencil drawings, therefore, the painter should copy mountains with exactitude, rather as if he were rendering a still life group. After absorbing the many possibilities of a mountain subject, you will be able to paint with emotional ease, knowing that you are prepared to express your feelings about the scene.

The demonstrations seen in Figure 8 show a systematic approach to the subject. At the top one sees how simple it is to paint mountains when the problem is approached from a practical standpoint. In this instance there are two mountain ranges, one in front of the other. The inexperienced student usually tries to paint an immediate passing effect of nature. This is not advisable; it is better to paint the two mountain ranges in one flat half tone, ignoring light and shadow and other dramatic effects. Here, the nearer range was thrown in deep shadow, *after* both were painted in one halftone. Little skill is required to do this, since the wetness of the preparatory ground enables the darker tone to merge with the lighter background. Although it is much deeper in tint, the dark-toned mountain range clearly belongs to the general effect. When painting dark trees with bushes or shrubs grouped in front, it is best to paint the whole ensemble in a dark vivid tone as seen in Figure 8. Then dip a clean rag in turpentine and suggest the bushes in front of the dark trees by washing out with the rag. This gives the feeling of diffused atmosphere and also the sensation of luminosity somewhat similar to pure water-color wash. It is comparatively easy to finish the dark trees and to paint the shrubs in front, suggesting a certain amount of detail in both.

Figure 8. Studies for **The Mountains of Arthog, North Wales**

Also in Figure 8 the foreground of rocks is boldly defined. It is better to accent their prismatic shapes rather than to allow a sloppy, soft formation. In the demonstration there was no attempt to make an accurate rendering of these rocks; rather, the story is told through sharp contours. All the shadows are painted on the left side of the rocks, the light source coming from the right.

Figure 9. The Mountains of Arthog, North Wales

This same demonstration is a study for the black and white picture entitled "The Mountains of Arthog, North Wales" (Figure 9)—an example of bold treatment. There is no blue sky in the original painting; it consists chiefly of silvery grays, with an occasional touch of yellow ochre and flake white to create an illusion of light and warmth. In order to suggest the solidity of mountains in oils I would advise that the first coat of color be kept deeper in tone than the actual subject; later it becomes relatively easy to add delicate tones.

The brushwork is easily recognizable in the reproduction, and the direction of the strokes indicates the modeling and strata of the various mountains. The strong brush marks were balanced to a certain extent by the smoothness of the water. A different style of brush handling was used in the immediate foreground and permitted a freedom of expression with no technical difficulty. The dark trees against the water provide a distinct section of the general scene. From the tonal standpoint they are valuable in sending the dark mountains into their correct aerial distance.

The painting entitled "Approach to the Adirondack Mountains" (Plate V) was principally concerned with the use of light-colored paint for sunlight on dark ground tints. Here, each brush stroke was important, particularly in showing light on the trees in the middle distance and on the roadway leading away from the foreground. All landscapes benefit when the sky becomes an integral part, but it must be correct in tone value or the whole subject will be disturbed. The warm-tinted foreground strikingly contrasts the blue-green elements spreading to the distance, while the dark trees on the right in the middle distance afford a subtle contrast to the distant range and therefore have a decisive pictorial value.

The observant artist is able to see many colors in nature. It is important to select from these only those which enhance the artistic motif of the picture. As a good test of technical ability, I suggest mixing oils out of doors so as to match nature's colors.

Plate V.
Approach to the
Adirondack Mountains

In the reproduction, "Mountains of California" (Figure 10), the tone values are clearly defined. The tall, dark fir trees near the foreground were painted broadly without much detail. They function well as part of the general composition, lending the correct tone values to the middle and distant mountains.

To paint mountains with success one must remember that, whatever the atmospheric condition during the painting, their weight and volume must be maintained. The distant range of mountains seen in Figure 10 shows solidity of form, although only slightly darker than the sky.

This picture depicts six different tone values in: 1) the sky, 2) the mountains adjoining the sky, 3) the range of mountains sweeping centrally across the composition, 4) the dark firs in the foreground, 5) the light sage brushes in the immediate foreground, 6) the material in and around these bushes.

In painting the foregrounds of landscapes, one has the opportunity to use really thick pigments. The thickness of oil paint pigment is by itself suggestive of the nearness of the foreground. To illustrate this point I have shown an example of the effect of thick pigment in the lower part of Figure 11, "Studies of Detail." The small bush formations are clearly delineated against the dark trees immediately behind. In the same illustration one can see the suggestion of a distant valley where the hill on the left is in shadow, while the hill on the right and the central hill behind show touches of light at their base, thus leading the eye up the valley.

Valleys vary greatly in kind. Some are broad and flat, curving gently up to wooded slopes at their sides; others are narrow and precipitous, with perhaps a stream running over a rocky bed down the center. Whatever type of valley one chooses as subject matter, it is of primary importance to establish broadly the general character of the scene within the framework of the canvas, searching above all for excellence of composition.

Figure 10. **Mountains of California**

Figure 11. Studies of Detail for **Mountains of California**

Figure 12. Basic Pattern of **The Old Warrior**

Figure 13. The Old Warrior

Technique—Waterside Scenery

The sense of atmosphere is essential in dealing with waterside subjects. To this end, the use of the palette knife is of great value, since it allows the artist to break away from rigid contours and suggest other possibilities that are less restrictive than those achieved with brushwork. Beautiful—and often unexpected—colors can be obtained with a knife. It is important, however, to diagnose the color composition in advance, in order to be sure that the various colors, however broadly applied to the canvas, will form part of a comprehensive design.

The expert in palette knife technique generally uses several knives to express pictorial subjects. A range of three different sizes is suggested; one, about seven inches long, the second, four inches, and the third, from two to three inches in length. Each knife must be flexible and must taper towards the end of the blade. Stiff or square-shaped blades are not conducive to good draftsmanship.

In the picture entitled "The Old Warrior" (Figure 13), there are various tones of red, with here and there a cooler tint. The student must have an intelligent comprehension of the subject if he wishes to succeed at marine painting. The problem demands rapid painting and clear perception. In the accompanying line drawing (Figure 12) little explanation is needed, since the various dotted lines show clearly how each portion of the total composition is interrelated in terms of the ships and the adjoining buildings.

For marine studies I advise students to paint freely and quickly, without worrying whether the drawing is good or bad. It is important, however, that those who wish to become expert in waterside scenery first make many pencil sketches of the subject, so that there is a store of accurate detail to draw upon.

The somewhat melancholy subject of "The Wreck, Gloucester Harbor, Massachusetts" (Figure 14) was interesting to paint because of its somewhat tragic theme. On completing an oil sketch I made a careful pencil drawing of the whole scene (Figure 15). The drawing suggested most of the details associated with age or antiquity in the old buildings; it indicated the nature of the broken woodwork and the various windows and doors. Students should remember that a pencil drawing can sometimes be more important than a color sketch, especially if, as in this instance, the final picture is painted away from the actual scene.

The colored reproduction entitled "The Harbor, Gloucester, Massachusetts," (Plate VI), was painted with a palette knife—except for a few minor touches. In the first stage the whole picture was covered by means of this interesting technique. The sharp thin lines of the rigging rising to the top of the masts were painted with a small sable brush. Experienced artists can use a very small palette knife for this purpose, but students are advised to use a brush.

Figure 14.   **The Wreck, Gloucester Harbor, Massachusetts**

Figure 15.   Pencil Drawing of **The Wreck, Gloucester Harbor, Massachusetts**

Plate VI.   The Harbor, Gloucester, Massachusetts

Figure 16.   Basic Pattern of **The Harbor, Gloucester, Massachuse**

The line drawing (Figure 16) conveys a clear conception of the basic pattern of this interesting marine subject. The two dark boats on the right afford a tonal balance to the deep shadow on the left, thrown by the stationary fishing boat alongside the harbor wall. The dotted lines emerging from the two dark-toned boats show how the eye is led into the picture, emphasizing the equally dark shadow. The flowing lines that spread from the fishing boat attract attention to the distant view.

Function of the Outdoor Sketch

A good way to approach the finished picture is to make not less than three outdoor sketches in color, in addition to pencil and charcoal drawings. This background of information gives the artist a chance to express his own personality, without losing the essential factors of the natural scene.

"The River, Menton, France" is shown in two colored reproductions. Plate VII represents the outdoor sketch and Plate VIII the finished picture. In making an outdoor sketch the main idea is to give prominence in form and color to the chief factor of interest. There are three important elements in Plate VII: the dramatic background of towering mountains, the warm-tinted buildings against the dark mountains, and the flow of the river from the foreground to the bridge and buildings on each side.

Plate VIII.   The River, Menton, France

Plate VII.   Sketch for **The River, Menton, France**

There is, of course, more drawing and more skill employed in the finished picture (Plate VIII). Both pictures were painted on Masonite, and on the extreme right-hand side of the outdoor sketch one can see several "bare spots" that show the actual color of the Masonite. The yellowish-brown of this board makes a good foundation color on which to paint a sketch or picture, and it is most helpful in assessing tone- and color-values while one is doing the painting. A white board or a canvas, on the other hand, demands more time, since it must be covered all over with oil colors before serious painting can be commenced.

Figure 17. San Juan Pueblo, New Mexico

In the case of "San Juan Pueblo, New Mexico" (Figure 17), representational painting, or painting precisely what one sees, was the main purpose. Nothing was altered or added in this subject, since nature had provided such a well-balanced composition. The central figure with the light cape hanging vertically downward accentuates—through contrast— the value of all the surrounding tones. The dark figure next to the central figure performs the same function.

The foliage at the top of the picture helps to frame the buildings below. But for this foliage it would have been necessary to paint in some clouds to achieve the framing effect, and this would have been somewhat unfortunate, since the tone value of the light clouds would have interfered with the light-colored buildings below.

The dark shadow at the foot of the picture—caused by a tree situated behind the artist—tends to emphasize the general composition of the whole subject. Another point of minor interest, though important to the composition, is the dark hill situated behind the light buildings and also the vertical poles cutting across the buildings and horizon; these belonged to the actual outdoor scene.

Development from an Outdoor Sketch

Building up a composition from a sketch should be—and generally is—a mental exercise free from the restrictions incurred in the making of an exact copy of nature. The arrangement of various natural components cannot fail to excite the mind of the creative painter who wishes to depict a coherent and understandable picture.

All good composition has a focal point, or center of interest, that plays an integral part in presenting the subject. To ensure success in the matter of composition, the various natural elements—whether of primary or secondary importance—must be controlled by the artist, and any naturalistic detail should be selected or rejected as required.

Students who paint woodland scenery often try to paint the subject as it appears to them, but they generally fail to capture the underlying spirit, or the mystery, of deep woods. The picture entitled "The Redwood Forest" (Figure 18) was a fairly accurate rendering of a natural arrangement of trees, foliage, light, and shadow. The figures in the central portion of the picture were included chiefly to indicate the height of the tall trees.

There is no conscious attempt in this painting to achieve a sense of poetry, or quietude, or any element of profound thought. It is fairly easy in outdoor sketching to render a woodland scene in outdoor color, but it is far more difficult to paint a picture that uses naturalistic forms to express the feelings of the artist.

Avoid painting a woodland scene that might be described as "a pretty picture." The artist's freedom as the designer of his picture provides the opportunity for the expression of his own artistic ego. The multiple colors of nature must be studied in order to build up strong compositions. Most people, unfortunately, appear to be content from observing only the obvious colors in a given landscape instead of the subtle colors that are comprised of a mixture of the primary colors. The only way to discover these colors is to study the effect of changing light during the day on certain outdoor objects, such as flowers, fields, grass, and so on. Those who take the trouble to do this cannot fail to see how ordinary natural subjects change their tints in the course of several hours.

Figure 18. The Redwood Forest

In the studio I tried several times to achieve a woodland scene of artistic interest. I painted a whole canvas with one tone only. While the paint was still wet, I dipped a small portion of a clean rag in turpentine and washed out some of the wet ground. I was thus able to suggest vertical passages of light. Figure 19 shows the result of this treatment. Using it as the basis for a picture, I made a similar composition, shown in the finished woodland study, Figure 20. The earlier illustration of the "Redwood Forest" (Figure 18) proved to be a helpful reference during the final painting. Notice that the light in Figure 20 is centralized in the composition. This striking effect is helped through contrast by the adjoining dark tree trunks on each side.

Figure 19. Suggestive Treatment of **Woodland Scene**

Figure 20. **Woodland Scene**—Finished Study

Plate IX.
A Dramatic Landscape

The colored reproduction, "A Dramatic Landscape" (Plate IX), was painted in the studio from an outdoor sketch. There was no attempt to get a "finished" painting, but rather to achieve a total freedom of expression.

In the finished color picture the blue river reflects the bluish sky and was painted simply, without stressing any naturalistic detail. Here also we see more of the width than is visible in the black and white reproduction. The dark clouds and sky are instrumental in showing the effect of sunlight on the nearer hills.

Plate IX was organized around the composition seen in Figure 21; here, more sky is shown, helping to give a dramatic effect of rain and windy weather. The river, being quiet in tone, gives a feeling of stability when compared to the wilder elements in the landscape. The low-lying hills and the dark trees at their base, as well as the arrangement of light in the foreground and on the distant hills, all play their part in expressing the composition of the whole subject.

Materials and Technique

In the selection of art materials, it is always advisable to buy the best. Aside from longer life, materials of good quality make it easier to acquire a good technique.

PALETTE. In general, the larger the palette, the better, since there is obviously more room for mixing colors and experimenting with various color blends. The palette should be well balanced and light in weight.

COLORS. Colors should be laid out on the palette in gradated tints from light to dark. The range should be from flake white to ivory black. Figure 22 shows the layout of colors in their proper order. Except for vermilion, each color is repeated several times in order to keep the colors pure and ready for blending during the painting of the picture.

The ten colors (including white) shown on the palette in Figure 22 are as follows: flake white, yellow ochre, light chrome, deep chrome, vermilion, alizarin crimson, deep ultra-marine blue, burnt sienna, and ivory black.

COLOR MIXING. It is advisable for the beginner to try numerous experiments in color mixing with red, blue, and yellow, since from these three colors, with the addition of white and black, a large number of different hues can be obtained, including a selection of subtle grays. The first experiment in color mixing should be tried with only black and white. Using four small areas of a canvas or board, mix black with a little white on the first area; then mix black with a little more white on the second area; the third and fourth areas should each receive proportionately more white. Thus the four areas will show four definite gradated tones of gray. These basic tints may now be systematically mixed with other colors, resulting in what should be a great variety of hues and tones.

There appears to be no end to the possibilities of color mixing. For further information on this subject I suggest you consult my book THE TECHNIQUE OF COLOR MIXING (Pitman), in which I have given a sound foundation as a basis for experimental color mixing.

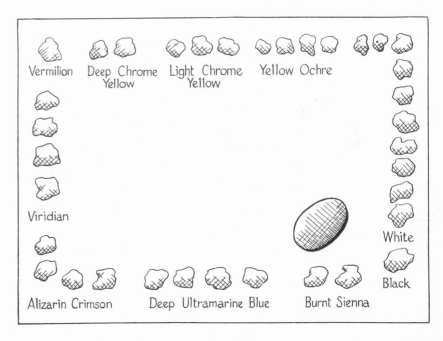

Figure 22. Palette with Color Arrangement

Vermilion   Deep Chrome Yellow   Light Chrome Yellow   Yellow Ochre

Viridian

Alizarin Crimson   Deep Ultramarine Blue   Burnt Sienna

White

Black

Figure 23.
First Series of Demonstrations

BRUSHES. The brush chiefly used for oil painting is the hog's-hair brush. Beginners should use one that is square in shape, so that the edges of pigment will be clear cut, as seen in Figure 23. At least ten brushes are necessary as preliminary equipment for painting. They should range in size from very small brushes up to those of an inch and a half in width.

Occasionally sable brushes may be used for delicate detail such as small branches of trees or shrubs, the rigging of ships, architectural details, and so on.

Oil brushes must be kept perfectly clean. The best method is to squeeze out the oil pigment on a piece of newspaper, then dip the brushes in paraffin or turpentine substitute, afterwards drying them with a clean rag. Finally, rub the brushes into a bar of ordinary soap, and then stir them well in very hot water. Repeat the soap-and-water process until they have no trace of paraffin or turpentine substitute.

CANVAS. There is a large variety of canvas grains, ranging from coarse to fine. The finer-grained canvas can be painted over with both thick pigment and delicately adjusted pigment, while on a coarse-grained canvas it is difficult to suggest a smooth surface.

It is well to prime one's own canvas. One coat of size is enough to prime a closely woven canvas. The paint will be matt in appearance if the priming is thin, and less matt in proportion as the priming is thicker. That is to say, the canvas is more or less absorbent according to the thickness of the priming.

Gelatine is the best all-around size, as it costs very little and is pure in content. It is easily prepared by dissolving in hot water. After the canvas is well sized with gelatine, a single layer of white lead can be lightly painted over the dry size. A coarse-fibred canvas takes a second layer of white lead—after the first coat has dried thoroughly. Formalin sprayed on the back of the canvas is sometimes used by artists as a preservative against dampness.

MASONITE. A useful and economical substitute for canvas is the material known as Masonite. It can be used for preliminary sketches, experimental work, and even for finished paintings. Masonite is smooth on one side and coarse on the other. Each side produces a different textural effect; however, the coarse side tends to absorb too much oil pigment, and thus it is often more advisable to build up one's own texture on the smooth side, as the occasion demands.

METHODS OF APPLYING THE PAINT. The first example in Figure 23, on the top left-hand side, shows oil-paint brush marks at varying angles. This method of application is the most essential technique in oil painting. The paintbrush should be well loaded with oil color before it is applied to the canvas.

The example in the top center of Figure 23 shows the result of painting pure white on top of a light-tinted ground. The wet ground modifies the brilliancy of the white paint. Any color painted over a wet surface always absorbs some of the ground color underneath.

The top right example is similar to the previous one. The ground tint is darker in tone than in the center demonstration. The horizontal brush lines were painted with white, thickly applied over the wet ground. (Thinly painted white over a dark ground is generally ineffective.)

The two lower examples demonstrate a feeling of movement. In each instance the ground color was painted quite flat, with no variation in tone. In the bottom left example horizontal lines with a wave-like motion were painted over the wet ground tint. Pure black was used at the lower end, and gradually lightened when approaching the distance, or higher portion, of the demonstration.

The last example was painted in a similar manner, with the addition of receding lines crossing horizontal lines approximately at right angles. Both of these examples suggest texture without using thick paint.

Figure 24.
Second Series of Demonstrations

In figure 24 the flat tone of the example on the top left-hand side was used also for the ground tint of the outer two studies. The example at the top right shows the effect of the palette knife used over a wet ground. Plenty of white oil paint is necessary for each flexible pressure of the knife on the canvas. In the lower example, no additional paint was required. The vertical lines on the left-hand side were made with a stiff hog's-hair brush that was continually cleaned with turpentine, in order to lift off the surface paint. A small brush was used for the thin vertical lines on the left, and a larger brush for the thicker lines. The zigzag vertical line and the light areas to the right were rendered with an ordinary linen rag dipped in pure turpentine. Some of the prepared ground color was wiped off to gain a more varied effect in tone.

The three demonstrations in Figure 25 show a method of suggesting lines by scraping off the surface paint with an ordinary penknife. The upper left demonstration is the flat ground color that was used as a basis for the two other demonstrations. In the second example the lines were made starting with a penknife from the lower part and working toward the higher. The third example used the same method, except that after the surface paint had been scraped off, white dots were added along the lines originally made by the penknife. The lower dots are larger than those higher, or further away. The smaller ones finally merge into the distance. On the right-hand side of this demonstration can be seen the effect of line treatment before the dots of white paint are added.

PALETTE KNIFE. A long, flexible knife is essential for mixing colors and for cleaning off the palette at the end of a day's work. Two or three additional palette knives are desirable for painting directly with the knife. These knives must be flexible enough for squeezing the color in any required direction. An example of palette-knife painting is shown in the upper right-hand corner of Figure 24.

MEDIA. Some knowledge of different oil media usually mixed with pigment is useful to the beginner. Generally, it is not necessary to use much additional medium in the paints, since there is plenty of oil mixed with the color pigment in the tubes. Pure spirits of turpentine makes an excellent mixture for painting because it evaporates, and consequently can do no damage to the permanency of pigments. Linseed oil helps to brighten the appearance of a painting, making it look more glossy than the average picture in which turpentine alone has been used. The volatile nature of turpentine leaves a matt or dry surface. Linseed oil should be used sparingly as a medium. About one-eighth linseed oil to seven-eighths turpentine is a fair proportion to work with. Too much linseed oil is liable to yellow the color of the pigments; also it takes a long time to dry.

As regards varnish, mastic varnish is generally used for protecting the surface of an oil painting. Before varnishing, care should be taken to warm the oil painting; otherwise an unpleasant "bloom" will be noticeable. No picture should be varnished until it has had at least three months to dry. If the oil pigment is thickly loaded, then not less than nine to ten months should elapse before varnishing. Mastic varnish is derived from mastic resin dissolved in spirits of turpentine, with a small quantity of oil added to give it some elasticity. After evaporation the varnish will leave a film of pure resin, which is highly protective to the painting underneath. Later, the resin surface becomes rather yellow in colour, and unless the painting has been placed under glass it not only collects dirt but is also susceptible to the sulphur acids of big cities. Mastic varnish eventually cracks, but is easily removed from the picture, which is the chief reason for its popularity.

Beeswax is another form of varnishing that deserves considerable attention. It can be removed quite as easily as mastic varnish, with the advantage of not yellowing as much; neither does it "bloom." So as to be able to apply it with a soft brush, pure turpentine should be added to make it liquid enough to handle with technical ease.

Figure 25.
Third Series of Demonstratio

Final Suggestions

Students are advised to sketch as much as possible, even if there is little time in which to do so. The main features of any subject are discovered through quick sketching. I have often advised my students to make as many as ten sketches for each finished outdoor painting. The final painting is ideally an accumulation of knowledge of detail gained from making quick studies.

It is likely that some particular passage in your subject matter will cause you difficulty—you may feel nervous about painting trees or water or the sky. The obvious thing to do in this case is to experiment with these problems separately until the nervousness is overcome. Be spontaneous in these studies. It does not matter if mistakes are made at the experimental level, since sketches are only the means to an end. Studies, moreover, can be stored away for future reference; in wintertime in your studio you can bring them out again and use the information they provide in some entirely different composition.

Failures should not be thrown away. Should a sketch—or even, a full work —fail to fulfill your expectations, save it, for it may teach you to avoid similar mistakes in composition or tone values in the future. It may even be possible to rescue the work with a turpentine rag by rubbing out the offending passage and repainting it as originally intended.

Once again I should like to emphasize the necessity of avoiding too much detail. Too many indiscriminate colors, too many ideas, invariably detract from the coherence of an artistic statement. Only after much experience in the technique of painting does one achieve the skill to suggest discreetly certain passages of detail.

With study and practice one is bound to develop the ability to balance the elements of color and form in the picture area. Once the technical facility is acquired, the artist must be wary of falling into a monotonous repetition of what is already known to him and easily expressed. Look at a scene before you as if you were seeing for the first time; in this way your work will always retain its original freshness.

Plate X.   Landscape, Elizabethtown, N. Y.